T0355866

INTERIOR
STYLE
japandi

INTERIOR
STYLE
japandi

KATHERINE MCLAUGHLIN

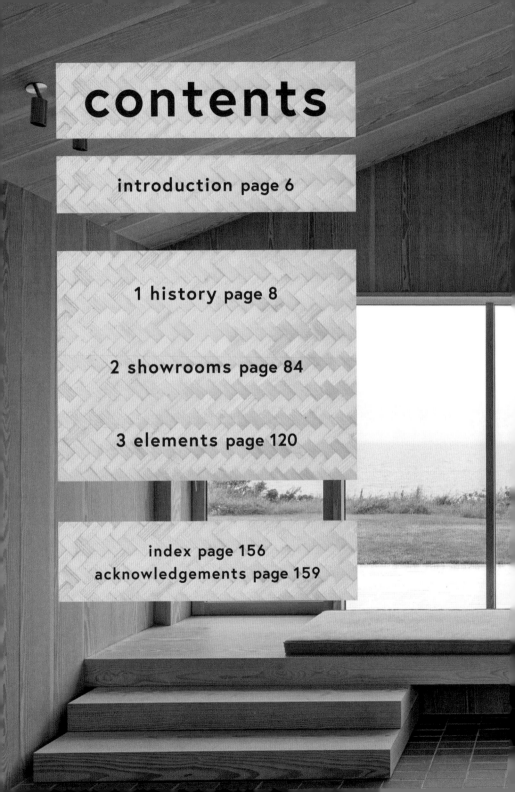

contents

The old adage "opposites attract" would lead one to believe that the best combinations in life are those that create the most beautiful friction: salty and sweet, yin and yang, sugar and spice. Japandi style, one of today's most popular interior design aesthetics, demonstrates that perhaps this isn't always the case. A portmanteau of Japanese and Scandinavian design, the look is a combination of the two culture's aesthetic sensibilities. However, it's not a forced merger. Both design philosophies share similar outlooks, emphasizing tranquil, minimal, functional interiors defined by clean lines and natural materials.

This book traces the history of Japanese and Scandinavian design to inform the modern genesis of Japandi style. We start in the 9th century in the Heian period of Japan, exploring everything from centuries-old castles in Kyoto to *wabi-sabi* and contemporary Japanese interiors. Then, we venture to Scandinavia, diving deep into modernism of the 20th century, World War Two's impact on the style, and Democratic Design.

Many people mark 2020 as the moment the term "Japandi" was coined, but the two cultures' association goes back much, much further. The Showroom section highlights striking examples of Japandi from around the world, followed by practical tips to incorporate the look into your home.

previous page *A simple but effective window seat in the Heatherhill Beach House, Denmark, designed by Norm Architects.*

right *A neutral and calm dining room, with stylish and practical built-in storage, natural materials and live stems.*

Japanese Interior Design History

The room is just over 80 square feet: straw mats cover the floor, soft sunlight breaks through paper screens in windows, a scroll depicting Zen Buddhist calligraphy hangs in a small alcove. A host rhythmically wipes a weathered bowl, from which steam from thick green tea escapes into the air. One by one, the vessel is passed to each guest to sip. Just outside, a faint breeze blows through the garden composed of stepping stones, lanterns and clusters of trees mirroring a natural landscape. Here, at a Japanese tea room, exists perhaps one of the fullest manifestations of traditional Japanese aesthetics.

The first half of the Japandi moniker, studying the history of Japanese design is an important step in understanding the combined style. In traditional Japanese residences, furniture

history

was sparse and interiors were often defined – and, by extension, decorated – by the structural elements of the building. For this reason, this section largely focuses on the country's historic architecture and how it relates to notable philosophies such as *wabi-sabi*.

However, Japan's history is extensive. Reliable records from the country date back as far as 400 CE, and this book does not cover every design achievement, style or milestone in the nation's lengthy chronicle. Instead, it attempts to trace the origin story of some of the most notable elements of Japanese design, such as *tatami* mats and *shoji* screens, to better inform the look known today as "Japanese" or "Japanese-inspired".

opposite *Traditional alcove in the Shiguretei Teahouse, Kanazawa, Japan.*

Shinden-zukuri Architecture

Traditional Japanese architecture draws inspiration from China, though much of it developed to address specific lifestyle and environmental conditions in the island nation. For example, Japanese summers are hot and humid, so traditional homes are often raised slightly so that air can move below them. The use of wood as a primary building material was not just an aesthetic choice, but rather because it can hold warmth in the winter, is cool in the summer, and more resilient to earthquakes. Historically, it was customary to sit on the floor, so Japanese design addresses this cultural norm.

To understand the country's historic architecture, it's important to journey back to the earliest emergence of a distinctly Japanese residential style. This can be largely traced to the Heian period (794–1185), when the Japanese missions to Tang China, which were efforts to learn Chinese customs and society, ended. While not the only factor, this supported

above *A wing of the Itsukushima Shrine, just off the coast of Hiroshima, Japan. The shrine was built according to* shinden-zukuri *style.*

the emergence of a distinctly Japanese culture known as *Kokufu bunka*, from which an architectural style known as *shinden-zukuri* arose. Referring mainly to nobility's mansion-estates of the period, many of the home's design characteristics became fundamental elements of Japanese architecture.

The style was defined by a *shinden*, a principal central structure, which connected via corridors to a number of secondary structures arranged in a U-shape. "A *shinden* wouldn't have a lot of internal divisions, and there weren't room dividers," explains Dr Alice Y. Tseng, a professor of Japanese art and architecture in the Department of History of Art and Architecture at Boston University. "It was mostly just one large, open interior space." These homes often featured *shitomi* (lattice shutters that hinge upwards), *sudare* (screens or blinds made from horizontal slats, usually bamboo or wood, woven together with string), and roofs made from organic materials such as thatch. "Compared to formal Chinese architecture, there was less paint on the wood and the roof covering would not be tile, which made it very different visually," Dr Tseng adds. "There was more emphasis on materials kept in their natural state."

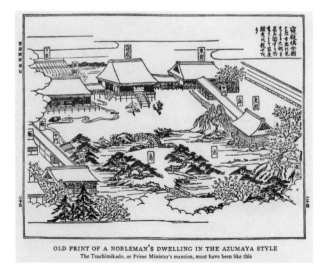

right *A drawing of* shinden-zukuri *style, with the primary hall and surrounding secondary structures. Taken from* Diaries of Court Ladies of Old Japan, *1920.*

OLD PRINT OF A NOBLEMAN'S DWELLING IN THE AZUMAYA STYLE
The Tsuchimikado, or Prime Minister's mansion, must have been like this

The gardens of these homes were also quite spectacular. Indeed, many of the buildings were designed to take advantage of these natural sites. At the time, Kyoto was the country's capital, and since summers were hot and humid, channels were dug to divert water throughout the city from a number of rivers. In aristocratic homes, streams called *yarimizu* were crafted to flow between buildings and throughout the garden. Some residences even had a pavilion that projected out over a lake and was connected to the mansion through covered walkways. A dry garden covered in white sand was often located between the pond and *shinden* and used for holding formal ceremonies.

The homes of common people included similar elements, but to a less opulent degree. "Ordinary houses had wooden doors and only a main building without extensions or pavilions," A. L. Sadler wrote in *Japanese Architecture: A Short History*. As Dr Tseng explains, a standard home might have been significantly smaller and would have used lower-quality materials. "Everyone would mostly be using wood for construction, but the quality and the type of wood would differentiate the high-level architecture versus regular homes," she says.

opposite top *Traditional wooden* shitomi *shutters.*

opposite bottom *A wooden* sudare *blind.*

Shoin-zukuri Architecture

As Japanese society, culture, and government changed, so
did its architecture. After the Heian period, a new
residential style known as *shoin-zukuri* emerged. It first
appeared in the Kamakura period (1192–1333), then evolved
in the Muromachi period (1338–1573). "As it developed,
shoin-style came to be associated with residential interiors of
the warrior class," Dr Tseng explains.

As described in *Japan in the Muromachi Age*, edited by John
Whitney Hall and Toyoda Takeshi, the Muromachi period was
unique in Japanese history, largely characterized by a time in
which new military aristocracy strived to model the lifestyle of
nobility. For this reason, many elements of *shinden* architecture
are present in *shoin* residences, though new developments were
also incorporated. As *shoin* architecture evolved, certain
inspiration from *shinden* architecture receded.

The style makes use of a more modest scale, solid wall
construction and sliding screens. Its name comes from a
formative element of the style, *shoin*, which derived from study
spaces used in Buddhist temples, and became more of a
reception area in *shoin-zukuri* buildings. This room would
include a built-in desk alcove (*tsuke-shoin*, or sometimes
referred to as simply *shoin*) with a *shoji* window (a wood lattice
frame covered with a translucent white paper) above it, a
tokonoma (a recessed alcove to display decorative art) and
chigai-dana (staggered shelves built into the wall).

It is also at this point that many distinctive elements of
Japanese design first emerged. "This is when we get the sliding
doors (*fusuma*) and fixed *tatami* mats," Dr Tseng explains.
"That didn't exist in *shinden*." (*Tatami* mats are rectangular mats
made from a straw base and woven rush cover, and while a
version did exist in *shinden* architecture, they were portable.)

Buildings in the style would be made primarily from wood
and often featured square pillars, coffered ceilings and wall
panels. To designate its significance, the primary room where

opposite *The wooden corridor
of Ninomaru Palace in Nijo
Castle, Kyoto, Japan.*

above *Exterior of Ninomaru Palace, Kyoto, Japan, built in the 17th century.*

overleaf *The* Ohiroma *in Nijo Castle.*

the *tsuke-shoin*, *tokonoma* and *chigai-dana* were located was often raised one step above the main floor.

In contrast to *shinden-zukuri*, "There were many different partitions and opportunities for decoration," Dr Tseng explains. The screens or sliding doors could be painted (often with nature scenes), and in major castles, a famous artist might be commissioned to do this. Furniture was used depending on occasion and might include pieces such as a low table or arm rest, which were then stored away when no longer needed. "There was no fixed heavy furnishing," Dr Tseng confirms. "It was very modular in that way." Depending on the owner, the residences could be very opulent or more subdued. For example, "You could dress up the wood with carvings if you wanted, or keep it in its natural state," Dr Tseng adds.

Ninomaru Palace, the main palace of Nijo Castle in Kyoto, is an incredible example of *shoin*-style design. Built at the beginning of the Edo period (1603–1867) under the first shogun (a military leader) of the Tokugawa line, Ieyasu (1543–1616), the interiors are incredibly symbolic. At this time, the shogun held significantly more power than the emperor, and the interiors of Ninomaru Palace, which are extremely opulent, were designed to demonstrate that control.

The structure is made up of connected buildings that are crafted from hinoki cypress. Inside, the rooms are defined by decorative panels featuring nature scenes, lavish gilding, lacquer and intricate wood carvings. *Tatami* mats cover the floors while *fusuma* doors grant access from one room to the next. The *Ohiroma* (the great hall) in Ninomaru features *tatami* mats across the floor, an intricate coffered ceiling, a *tokonoma*, *chigai-dana*, and a writing desk alcove. When hosting an audience with his subjects, the shogun would sit in the section of the room that was higher, designating his status.

The Emergence of *Wabi-sabi*

I t was around this time, when *shoin*-style design was developing, that the beginnings of an aesthetic concept now known as *wabi-sabi* first appeared. Many aspects of the philosophy derive from Buddhist teachings, but its history in Japanese society generally traces back to another important aspect of Japanese culture: tea.

In the 12th century, a Japanese monk named Myōan Eisai (1141–1215), travelled to China to study through the Línjì school, a sect of Chan Buddhism. When he returned to his native land, he brought back both the religious practice he had learned – in Japan, this school of Buddhism became known as Rinzai – and tea seeds to the country. While there are records that show the steeped drink was consumed in the country as early as the 8th century, this was largely the genesis for what would become *chanoyu*, the Japanese tea ceremony, or "the way of the tea".

Eisai introduced a unique style of tea preparation, in which tea is ground into a fine powder – matcha – and combined with hot water to make a beverage. During this time, monks used the drink to help them stay awake during meditation. Tea also made its way into aristocratic homes, where it was consumed at loud parties in displays of wealth. Precious utensils, often imported from China, were used, and guests would guess the origins of different teas.

All of this changed in the 15th century when Zen Buddhist masters reformulated tea into a humble practice designed to be spiritually uplifting. A tea master named Murata Jukō (1423–1502) is generally credited as the practice's founder. Breaking tradition, Jukō served tea to aristocrats using locally made, accessible and understated utensils, crafting a style of the tea ceremony that came to be known as *wabi-cha*. According to the Ministry of Foreign Affairs in Japan, *wabi* means "desolation", but the Zen perspective understands this positively. In this view, "the greatest wealth is found in desolation and poverty, because we look inside ourselves and find true spiritual wealth there when we have no attachments to material things," the agency explains. Today, the word is sometimes translated to "simple" or "humble".

Notably, many historians also trace the *wabi-sabi* philosophy to this point in history. "When *wabi-sabi* was first conceived, it was meant to be in contrast to a very perfect Chinese style of tea," Dr Tseng says. "There was also a strong connection to Buddhist ideology and teachings to step away from material goods and things that are superficially perfect."

Today, it is often described as the acceptance of imperfect things, and perhaps more importantly, a celebration of the inherent beauty found in imperfect things. The phrase is a combination of two words: *wabi* (desolation, simplicity) and *sabi*, which is generally understood as the notion that beauty comes from age.

However, Dr Tseng says that it's worth noting that "the aesthetic was based on very elite people's understanding of what being humble was about. It was not created by people who were actually humble or poor. It's a rich person's perception of what it feels like or looks like to work with the most minimal resources."

While some view *wabi-sabi* as a purely visual philosophy, it is broader than this and can be applied to many facets of life. Nonetheless, as Leonard Koren explains in *Wabi-Sabi for Artists, Designers, Poets & Philosophers*, "it reached its most comprehensive realization within the context of the tea ceremony." This largely happened in the 16th century, when the tea ceremony was perfected and turned into an art form.

above *A Japanese couple in a traditional teahouse.*

The Tea Ceremony and *Wabi-sabi* in Architecture

Today, a tea ceremony is about more than just a drink, but rather a ritual that includes architecture, interior design, flower arranging, food preparation and performance. A formal ceremony is a four-hour gathering in which a host prepares and serves green tea to guests. The host or hostess often spends decades studying not only tea and its preparation, but also learning to appreciate art, poetry, flower arranging and how to care for a garden.

The ceremony is designed to humble participants and focuses on "the profound beauty of the simplest aspects of nature – such as light, the sound of water and the glow of a charcoal fire (all emphasized in the rustic tea hut setting)," the Ministry of Foreign Affairs of Japan explains in a fact sheet about the ceremony. There is also a focus on human endeavour and the beauty this can create, which may manifest in objects or tea utensils. Though different schools of thought and iterations have developed over the years, most tea ceremonies share this common goal – all thanks to a man named Sen no Rikyū.

The son of a rich merchant, Rikyū was born in 1522 in Sakai, just outside of Osaka. His upbringing afforded him opportunities to experience the aristocratic version of a tea ceremony, but he was more interested in the Zen way. Rikyū appreciated the way Buddhist monks approached the ceremony as a way to celebrate the sacred nature of everyday life and was inspired by Jukō's example. During his lifetime, he redefined nearly every aspect of the tea ceremony, including the utensils and procedures, but perhaps most importantly for the context of this book, he designed and developed monumental teahouse architecture. In Japanese, these structures are called *chashitsu*.

His aesthetic called for a smaller tea room – at its smallest, one that was just six feet square and would fit two *tatami* mats (previously, four and a half *tatami* mats were common). He was the first person to build a structure dedicated to tea alone (instead of using a room in the house) and preferred unaltered natural materials, such as bamboo or gourd vases. Among the most notable design elements was a "crawling entrance", which required anyone who entered to either do so on their knees or bow their heads, eliminating markers of class or rank.

Once inside, the space was little more than the walls of the structure and the mats on the floor, the only decoration a scroll or vase with flowers in the *tokonoma*. This minimalism was Rikyū's way of putting focus on the practice, the guest, and encouraging those inside to appreciate the simple beauty of the world around them. He stripped nearly everything non-essential from the tea ceremony, and as *Encyclopedia Britannica* explains, "firmly established the concepts of *wabi* (deliberate simplicity in daily living) and *sabi* (appreciation of the old and faded) as [the ceremony's] aesthetic ideals."

above *A portrait of Sen no Rikyū, 16th-century Japanese tea master, considered the historical figure with the most profound influence on the Japanese "way of tea".*

Tai-an, a teahouse at Myokian Temple in Oyamazaki, Kyoto, is considered the only extant *chashitsu* Rikyū designed. The structure, which was built in the 16th century, is now a Japanese National Treasure. Featuring a bamboo frame, mud walls and *shoji* windows, it is an extremely small tea room, only large enough for the host and one guest.

Inside, the space holds two *tatami* mats and a *tokonoma*. The interior walls are textured; the humble mud enclosure does not pose as anything it's not. The windows, which are irregular in both size and placement (an architectural breakthrough of the time), show an unparalleled command of natural light. As sunlight enters the room through the *shoji*, it creates softly diffused light, subdued pockets of illumination and patches of shadows.

Kengo Kuma, one of the most prolific Japanese architects working today, wrote about Tai-an in his 2013 book *Small Architecture*. "You won't understand what Tai-an is all about until you actually crawl into this small box and experience the very moment when the building, which is almost as small as your body, starts dissolving and enveloping your body softly and lightly, as if it were your clothes," he explained.

Built during the Azuchi-Momoyama period (1574–1600), a time when *shoin* style architecture was still in fashion, Tai-an is perhaps the best representation of the *wabi-sabi* philosophy: a humble and purposeful space, leaving nothing to be desired yet offering no more than necessary. Beauty is found within nature and the simple pleasures to be experienced inside. Contemporary interpretations of the look often seek to replicate this humble and simplistic elegance.

Sukiya-zukuri Architecture

By the 16th century, tea masters became heavily influential in the world of domestic architecture, interior decoration and garden design. In fact, Encyclopedia Britannica credits the "simple grace" of many Japanese interiors to hereditary tea families and schools.

In the Edo period (1603–1867), the final period of traditional Japan, a new style of residential architecture emerged that was based on teahouse architecture. Called *sukiya-zukuri*, natural timber was the main construction material, sometimes with the bark still on. Harmony with nature was among the primary goals of the aesthetic, which was achieved through rustic simplicity.

As architect and architectural historian Terunobu Fujimori wrote in his 2017 book *Japan's Wooden Heritage: A Journey Through a Thousand Years of Architecture,* shoin and *sukiya* styles of architecture share many characteristics and can be difficult to differentiate. "In their basics the two styles are similar – both have *tokonoma* alcoves, *tatami* mats, *fusuma* sliding doors and *shoji* sliding screens – but leave very different impressions," he

opposite *Tai-an teahouse in Kyoto, Japan.*

below *The interior of a traditional Japanese teahouse.*

explains. *"Shoin* has a rigid, assertive formality while *sukiya* is more supple and slender." Further, *sukiya* style often features smaller rooms.

The Katsura Imperial Villa in Kyoto is regularly touted as the epitome of *sukiya* style. An imperial residence originally belonging to the noble Hachijō-no-miya family, *sukiya* aesthetic can be seen throughout the complex, but most notably in the Koshoin, Chushoin and Shingoten, the main residential structures. Beams are unfinished – some even appear to be untouched logs – and there is no gilding or decorative accents. According to the Ministry of Foreign Affairs of Japan, not only is the complex the "finest extant example" of the style, but it is also "famous for its harmonious blending of buildings with the landscape garden".

opposite *View of the garden through a teahouse at Katsura Imperial Villa, Kyoto, Japan.*

Contemporary Japanese Interior Design

Now, Japanese design combines elements of Western influence with traditional practices to create an aesthetic that is familiar to foreigners but still distinctly of the native country. In the mid-1800s, Japan underwent a period of extreme Westernization as part of the Meiji era (1868–1912), which influenced many elements of Japanese culture and brought forth political, economic and social changes. Japanese citizens studied Western customs, and international design movements made their way to Japan. Later, Japanese architects and designers developed their own unique contemporary practices, such as the Metabolism movement after World War Two.

Comparing Shinjuku City in Tokyo – full of nightclubs, karaoke bars and neon signs – with the Japanese countryside, where it's still common to find wood residences built in traditional styles, proves the breadth and variety of Japanese design today. Ultimately, what could be defined as "Japanese design" is not one singular answer.

But when speaking about a distinct interior design style, Japanese interiors are often described similarly. It's an aesthetic focused on serene, minimalistic and organic construction. There is a practical approach to the room's layout, often centred on a "less is more" ideology.

The colour palette in modern Japanese design is usually very neutral and makes use of earth tones, such as browns and creams, with green as an accent. Overall, the hues are muted and subdued. Furniture is crafted in natural materials, such as solid wood, and features clean lines and a sleek profile. Other materials found throughout the space include stone, paper and glass, which could be seen in architectural elements like doors, walls or windows, or could enter the design via decorative objects. That said, most decoration is both functional and beautiful and may include pieces such as bowls, vases or teapots.

Additionally, a dialogue with the natural world is often

opposite *A contemporary interpretation of traditional Japanese design in the T3 House, designed by CUBO design architects. Historical features, such as the paper* shoji *screens, are brought into the 21st century.*

evident. This could be through large floor-to-ceiling windows that bring the outside world in, or the thoughtful addition of plants, such as bonsai trees or moss. Because Japanese interiors are generally less embellished, much of the visual interest is created through texture. For example, the rough character of a jute rug inspired by a *tatami* mat may juxtapose against a nearby tree leaf, which is waxy and smooth. Rattan, bamboo, silk, cotton and ceramics are also common textures featured in Japanese interiors.

Though there is a notable connection to nature, lines remain clean instead of organic. Right angles – whether through rugs, furniture, or square lattice frames on screens – are defining elements of the look. Homes in this style often avoid clutter by utilizing smart storage solutions and, where possible, reduce furnishing to the essentials. To recall traditional elements of Japanese interiors, some designers include sliding doors, *shoji* screens or paper lanterns. Artwork in muted tones that depict aspects of the natural world or a landscape can also inspire a connection to the traditional design ethos.

right *A contemporary renovation of a Japanese house in Osaka, Japan, by Hiroto Kawaguchi.*

Scandinavian Design

On 15 January 1954, the Virginia Museum of Fine Arts (VMFA) in Richmond celebrated the opening of its latest exhibit with a dinner party full of diplomats. Ambassadors from Denmark, Sweden, Norway and Finland were in attendance to commemorate a new show spotlighting a growing movement in the art world. In a note to the museum's board of trustees, Henry W. Anderson, the president of the group, explained that "the display will present to the people of America the truly fine objects for the home being produced today by the people of Scandinavia. Beautifully designed furniture, textiles, silver, glass, and china, both handmade and machine done, will be shown." Titled Design in Scandinavia, the exhibition space held over 700 homewares: leggy, streamlined chairs crafted in wood sat on risers, sleek pendant lights dangled from the ceiling, unfussy window treatments hung from rods.

In some ways, the displayed furniture was similar to the pieces mid-century designers were already creating (think the likes of Charles and Ray Eames, Florence Knoll, Marcel Breuer or Frank Lloyd Wright). There was a noticeable emphasis on clean lines, minimal ornamentation and simple forms. However, there were also many differences: where other Western designers experimented with steel, glass and plastic – at the time, new and innovative materials – these were largely absent in the Scandinavian counterparts. Nordic pieces showcased a greater emphasis on negative space: long legs and open chair backs created an unbarred and airy profile. The designs also demonstrated a softer, lighter and more neutral colour palette. There was emphasis on "exquisite, though not necessarily elaborate items," Betty Pepis, a reporter for The New York Times, wrote in an article about the show.

The public was hooked. After closing at VMFA, the exhibit travelled throughout the USA and Canada for nearly four years and was shown at over 20 additional museums. Interest in this new take on design disseminated widely, and the style came to be known as Scandinavian Modern.

above *Chairs on display at the Design in Scandinavia exhibition, 1954.*

What is Scandinavian Design?

In many parts of the world, referencing "Scandinavian design" does not refer to things made in Scandinavia, but rather a specific design movement that happened in the early to mid-20th century. At this time, many changes were occurring in the Western world. Social reforms, technological and scientific advances, and economic growth brought forward new perspectives, and designers were eager to express this through their creative disciplines. Enter modernism. In broad strokes, the movement – which spread through visual arts, architecture and interior and product design, among other subjects – saw an emphasis on experimentation, while unnecessary ornament was simplified and functionality was prioritized over aesthetics.

Modern Nordic design, not to be confused with contemporary Nordic design, developed in tandem with this broader Western movement (though it was called

above *A Danish-designed suite of furniture with wooden arms and striped wool fabric, from an issue of* Housewife *magazine, 1955.*

opposite *A special-edition wishbone chair, released in 2024 by Carl Hansen & Søn, to mark what would have been the 110th birthday of celebrated Danish designer Hans Wegner. Originally designed in 1949, the iconic chair has been in continuous production.*

functionalism in the region). While designers shared similar philosophies as their contemporaries in other nations, they were creating under different circumstances. Most notably, Scandinavian designers often strived to maximize light, understandable in a region known for long winters and short days.

The fact that the Scandinavian style of modernism is often described as cool, clean, cozy and streamlined is no accident. "Historically, the colour palette celebrated dusty and warm hues yet with an eye to the bigger world," says Thomas Lykke, co-founder and head of design at OEO Studio in Copenhagen. The hues "enhanced light yet also add warmth, contrast and boldness".

Furniture is leggy and open, often crafted from woods such as birch, ash and teak. Chairs feature little upholstery, as pieces were designed so light would bounce off them – walls and floors are often pale for the same reason. Spaces are minimal, uncluttered and architecturally designed to maximize sun: large windows, minimal drapery and organic materials are often hallmarks of the look. Even before the modernist movement, Nordic countries prioritized quality craftsmanship, which often carried forward in this new era as well. After years of gradual build-up in the home countries and abroad, the style reached peak mass appeal in the 1950s and 60s, thanks in large part to exhibits like Design in Scandinavia.

Nonetheless, this is still a generalized description. As modernism spread throughout the Western art and design world, it developed differently in each Nordic country. When Design in Scandinavia opened at the Brooklyn Museum in April 1954, a press release for the show did record some of these variations. "Design in Scandinavia has been made lively and stimulating through the juxtaposition of the self-revealing arts and crafts of four mature, happily individualized nations," the release stated. Organizers for the exhibition pointed to the displayed chairs as evidence of this.

"The Danish chairs, with their intricate workmanship and highly sculptured surfaces, come from a country where hand operations in small shops are very much the rule. In contrast, the Swedish chairs are more frequently designed for factory production," the release continued. Both were equally

successful but demonstrated different perspectives and economic circumstances. Other variations could be seen in the fabrics. Norwegian upholstery materials were more vivid in colour and displayed contrast between light and dark, whereas Finnish fabrics were defined by more muted hues.

Even so, these attempts to delineate between countries and national aesthetics didn't trump the fact that it was all presented together under the name "Scandinavian Design". Decades later, this is still how many recognize the style. But the moniker falls short in many ways. "It's not a perfect term," says Dr Monica Obniski, a design historian and curator of decorative arts and design at the High Museum of Art in Atlanta, Georgia. She previously worked at the Milwaukee Art Museum, where she co-curated an exhibit in collaboration with the Los Angeles County Museum of Art titled Scandinavian Design and the United States, 1890–1980.

It's like describing both the beach houses of Los Angeles and the high-rises of New York City as "American" while simultaneously assuming that these are the only two design styles in the United States. It could be true to a certain extent, but it's an extremely broad descriptor for a relatively narrow design ethos. After all, it's not as if every craftsperson from the European region in the 20th century created work in the functional, modern style that today is called "Scandinavian". As Dr Obniski explains, "It doesn't acknowledge vernacular wares or the work of indigenous people, among other things." What's more,

Iceland and Finland aren't even Scandinavian countries, but Nordic ones. So why did it all get lumped together as one look? And a uniquely Scandinavian one?

A Distinctly Scandinavian Aesthetic

According to Kerstin Wickman, a Scandinavian design expert, World War Two was the culprit. As she explained in a 1996 article titled "Scandinavian Design: The Dream is Still Alive", at the onset of the global conflict designers from other Nordic countries fled their native lands for neutral Sweden, where they met and learned from the creatives there. "The true impetus," Wickman wrote, "was the closeness of a group of Scandinavian designers and architects, all with their roots in International Modernism."

This geographic proximity certainly helped cultural exchange, but many scholars also acknowledge that there was a politically strategic motive too. As a 2016 long-form article published on Curbed described it, the movement could be seen as a "major international PR campaign". Following World War Two, there was a concerted effort from advertisers, museums and the media in both Europe and the United States to push a homogenous "Scandinavian" style. "There were many actors in the United States that really wanted this to take place," Dr Obniski explains.

In a still-recovering, post-war world, the idea of a peaceful, neutral, egalitarian place like the Nordic countries was an incredibly powerful marketing tool. Buying "Scandinavian" products allowed consumers to feel like they were aligning their values with these same ideals, and exhibitions like Design in Scandinavia, advertisements and other media were designed to subtly encourage this messaging.

According to historian Widar Halén, this wasn't a one-sided effort. As he writes in the book *Scandinavian Design: Beyond the Myth* (co-edited with Wickman), Nordic countries held a series of conferences throughout the 1940s about their cooperation and solidarity, and resolved that they "could be perceived as an entity when it came to design issues".

These countries banded together under the aegis of Design in Scandinavia, because none of them had the resources to sustain the marketing push or consumption rate of the American marketplace alone. Indeed, as Anderson, the president of the board of trustees at VMFA, wrote in his letter, the exhibit had been financed by Norway, Sweden, Finland and Denmark. The specific aesthetic we now call Scandinavian carries that name because that's how it was communicated to consumers in the United States, the UK and other countries. And decision-makers specifically chose to do it this way because this branding was approachable, easily digestible and based on the perception of a better world.

above *Front cover of the Design in Scandinavia catalogue.*

"Even in putting together our exhibition, we knew the regional limitations of the term 'Scandinavian Design'," Dr Obniski adds. "But some still use the name because it really had a cultural cachet in the post-World War Two era." Many designers and design-lovers still use the phrase "Scandinavian" to describe pieces either from the movement or inspired by it.

In some ways, this can make the style feel fabricated, but it doesn't discredit the far-reaching impact the actual products and spaces had on the design world. Many of the most famous designs from the movement are still in production because they are timeless, functional and beautiful pieces. But for better or worse, if you close your eyes and picture "Scandinavian" design, there's a reason your imagination will likely take you to a birch armchair before a Norwegian rosemaled bowl or a Swedish Dala horse.

opposite *Hans Wegner's Round Chair, 1949.*

above *The Egg Chair, originally designed by Arne Jacobsen, styled by Fritz Hansen.*

Scandinavian Designers

t was ultimately the visionary architectural, product and
furniture designers of the era who defined what would come
to be known as the Scandinavian design movement. Though
countless names could be included in this list, the following
represent some of the biggest players in the movement. They
designed different types of products, but each brought new
perspectives and were collectively revered for their take on
simple, functional pieces.

Hans Wegner

Hans Wegner's (1914–2007) style is most often described as
"organic functionality". The Dane is known for his furniture
designs, particularly his chairs, many of which were made from
wood. Some of his most notable pieces include the Round
Chair (1949) and the Wishbone Chair (1950). In 1960,
Wegner's Round chairs received even more public attention
when they were used as seating during the first televised US
presidential debate between John F. Kennedy and Richard
Nixon. "Many foreigners have asked me how we created the
Danish style," Wegner has been quoted as saying. "I've
answered that it was a continuous process of purification and
simplification – to cut down to the simplest possible design of
four legs, a seat and combined back and armrest."

Arne Jacobsen

Known for his contributions to architectural functionalism, Arne
Jacobsen (1902–71) was among the most prolific designers of
the Scandinavian modern movement. In addition to buildings,
he, like Wegner, was celebrated for his chairs. In 2002, *The New
York Times* described Jacobsen as the "Frank Lloyd Wright of
Denmark: a prolific, versatile and talented architect and designer
who has been revered more after his death than he ever was in
life". The paper referred to him as the "father of Danish
modernism", and he was particularly interested in affordable

above *The Paimio Armchair, designed by Alvar Aalto, 1932.*

design for the masses. The Egg and Ant Chair are among his most popular designs and are both still in production.

Alvar Aalto

Alvar Aalto (1898–1976) worked across disciplines including architecture, furniture, glassware, textiles and even town planning. The Finnish visionary designed all of the furniture for his buildings and sought to synthesize aesthetic and practical standards. He was known to take a humanistic approach to work and often prioritized psychological needs in his designs, such as colour, sound, material and light. "In the 1930s, Aalto became identified with wood – the essential, profuse, natural material that served as the backbone of the Finnish economy – and known for his explorations of bending and shaping it," the Museum of Modern Art in New York explains on its website. His most recognizable work is the Paimio Armchair, designed between 1931 and 1932, which was made from a singular piece of plywood that appears to float in its frame. Aalto created the chair for the Paimio Tuberculosis Sanatorium, and its angled back was intended to make breathing easier for patients.

Greta Magnusson-Grossman

Before rising to fame in the Los Angeles design scene, Greta Magnusson-Grossman (1906–99) was heavily influenced by her homeland, Sweden. She cut her teeth working as an apprentice at furniture manufacturer Kärnans and completed a fellowship at Stockholm arts institution, Konstfack, before moving to Los Angeles with her husband during World War Two. Here, the couple established the Magnusson-Grossman Studio. Throughout her career, she worked as an architect and furniture and interior designer and was heavily influenced by the European modernism movement. The Gräshoppa Floor Lamp is one of her most recognizable designs and features a tripod base and notable backward tilt.

above *The Gräshoppa Floor Lamp, 1947.*

opposite *Finnish architect Eliel Saarinen, 1873–1950.*

Eliel Saarinen

Born in Finland, architect Eliel Saarinen (1873–1950) emigrated to the United States with his family in 1923. As the first president of the Cranbrook Academy of Art in Bloomfield Hills, Michigan, he is often credited with influencing modernism in the United States and was crucial to American's interest in Scandinavian design. Much of the school's teaching staff was from Finland and Sweden, and their work imbued curiosity about Scandinavian styles in the USA. He often worked with his son, Eero Saarinen, who was also an immensely influential architect in the middle of the 20th century.

Design Research

In addition to exhibits, stores also played a major role in introducing the Scandinavian aesthetic to American consumers, and none more so than Design Research (D/R). Generally credited as the originator of the lifestyle store concept, it was founded in 1953 by architect Ben Thompson and sold furniture, décor, accessories and even clothes. "Simply put, D/R is a General Store of good design," Thompson synthesized in the company's 1968 Christmas catalogue.

The original D/R store was located in Cambridge, Massachusetts, but the business expanded to a mini chain by the mid-1960s with outposts in a number of major cities in the USA. Inside, shoppers could find products from leading modernist designers, particularly those from Europe such as Marcel Breuer (Hungarian-German) and Joe Colombo (Italian), though notably it also carried a great Scandinavian stock, including work from Hans Wegner and Alvar Aalto.

"Ben introduced the work of some designers established in Scandinavia for decades, plus a new generation of Europeans, premiering and promoting each product as a major news event for American consumers," Jane Thompson and Alexandra Lange wrote in their 2010 book *Design Research: The Store That Brought Modern Living to American Homes*.

Further, D/R was the exclusive US representative for Marimekko, a Finnish clothing and textile brand. In 1960, Jackie Kennedy famously wore a Marimekko dress on the cover of *Sports Illustrated*, which she purchased at D/R. Soon after, the brand skyrocketed in popularity.

"Without question, D/R was the most influential force in 20th-century America in creating an awareness and appreciation for modern design in the consumer world," Rob Forbes, the founder of Design Within Reach wrote in the foreword to Thompson and Lange's book.

Thompson started the store hoping to show that well-designed products could improve people's lives. Unfortunately, the business closed in 1979 but nonetheless had a substantial impact on the dissemination and appreciation of Scandinavian design. In a 1979 *New York Times* story about the business's closing, the paper described the store: "From unadorned glassware to Marimekko print dresses, rugs and furniture, the Design Research style became synonymous with fresh, modern, functional design."

opposite *Exterior of the Design Research (D/R) store in Cambridge, Massachusetts, USA.*

above *Stock in the Design Research (D/R) warehouse.*

Democratic Design

"Democratic" is among the most popular adjectives used to describe Scandinavian design while simultaneously being the most difficult to tangibly define. After all, what *actually* makes a chair or table – or even an entire house – democratic?

In simple terms, the concept can be viewed as a "people-first" design philosophy that considers accessibility and functionality for a whole range of users. Take Jackie Kennedy's Marimekko dress. The Finnish company famously designed free-flowing pieces with simple cuts intended to encourage movement and accommodate many different body types, a concept that wasn't commonplace at the time.

IKEA, perhaps the most famous furniture company to come out of Scandinavia, is a leading contemporary advocate and practitioner of the concept. "Democratic Design is a tool we use when we develop and evaluate the products we put into our range," the company explained in a blog post. There are five factors to consider – function, form, quality, sustainability and low price – and, for IKEA, democratic design is achieved when there is a balance between all of them. Though popularized by the Swedish powerhouse, it's an idea that is deeply entrenched in the design philosophy of many Nordic countries.

Countries in the region have long been celebrated as egalitarian cultures, where all people are equal. "Being democratic in that kind of context is almost a given," Dr Obniski says. Known as social democracies and the epitome of the modern welfare state, the idea of accessible, good design that helps all people is imbued in the culture of these countries. "The designers saw it as their task to satisfy the needs of all social groups, especially the disadvantaged," Wickman, the Scandinavian design expert, explained in her article about the Scandinavian modern movement.

Arne Jacobsen was a leading pioneer of Democratic Design. Much of his work was informed by his "mathematical" design

philosophy: "economy plus function equals style". In 1952, Jacobsen released one of his most iconic designs, the Ant Chair, manufactured by Fritz Hansen and made from a shell of laminated plywood and three slim steel legs (later four legs). "I looked at the need: what sorts of chairs are needed? I saw a use for a new chair type for the small, combined kitchen and dining spaces that are now common in most new builds: a small, lightweight, affordable chair," Jacobsen told Danish newspaper *Information* in 1952. It was a design problem for which many of his contemporaries also strived to address.

The Ant Chair debuted in the cafeteria of pharmaceutical company NOVO Nordisk's Frederiksberg building, which Jacobsen designed. "Furthermore, I designed [the Ant Chair]

opposite *An illustration from a Dutch interiors magazine, 1960, showcasing bold colours and practical furnishings.*

so it could be used in canteens, for example, as a stacking chair. You can stack it by sliding the chairs together, which saves both time and labour," Jacobsen told *Information*.

The Ant represented a major moment in design history and took over a year to conceive. Using plywood was perhaps the most vital breakthrough: because it bends, the seat and back could be a single piece. The wild success of the Ant Chair inspired Jacobsen to continue developing similar seats, called shell chairs, which ultimately led to his Series 7 Chair, arguably one of his most famous designs.

But this wasn't the only example of the Danish architect's commitment to accessible creations. In 1957, Jacobsen released a line of cutlery, only instead of crafting it from traditional silver, he opted to make the utensils from stainless steel. Not only did this ensure the quality remained substantial, but it

retained the overall aesthetic of standard flatware. "I have had the idea for this cutlery for the past 20 years," he told the Danish newspaper *Berlingske Aftenavis* in 1958. "I was involved in shaping it in the workshop, snipping and cutting until the cutlery met the aesthetic and functional requirements." Later, in 1967, he released a tableware series called the Cylinda Line, which also employed stainless steel as a lower-cost alternative to silver.

However, Democratic Design extends beyond just affordability. "Interest in the everyday needs of the disabled and those with other handicaps as well as those on the factory floor has always been far greater in Scandinavia than elsewhere," Wickman explained. While it was introduced later in the Scandinavian modern movement, Swedes Maria Benktzon and Sven-Eric Juhlin's Kitchen Knife and Cutting Board is a

left *The Ant Chair by Arne Jacobsen, 1952.*

above opposite *Stainless steel cutlery by Jacobsen, 1957, styled by Georg Jensen.*

fantastic example of accessible design. The knife handle is large and angled while the cutting board includes partitions to safely guide the blade. The pair studied hand ergonomics in depth while crafting the product, which was intended to be easier for elderly citizens as well as those with disabilities to use. More broadly, the two were founding members of Ergonomi Design Gruppen, later renamed Veryday, an industrial design consultancy, which specialized in assistive devices, among other products.

In 1988, the Museum of Modern Art in New York held an exhibition titled Designs for Independent Living, which included products "for the aging and physically disabled". It's not surprising that a press release for the exhibition noted that most of the items displayed were "on loan primarily from Sweden".

Hygge

Though *hygge* is technically a Danish concept, it's often presented as a core element of the overall Scandinavian style. Pronounced "hoo-ga", it is usually described as a state of coziness, contentment and comfort, although there is no direct translation of the word into English.

"Hygge is often about informal time together with family or close friends," explains the Ministry of Foreign Affairs of Denmark in a blog post. The setting is often a home or comfortable location and could include sharing a drink or food with loved ones. "There is no agenda," the post continues, and according to the Danish government, winter is a prime time for hygge.

"Sitting around a bonfire making pancakes with friends can be hygge, but it is also as much about the atmosphere and the energy as much as the setting" Lykke, the Copenhagen-based designer at OEO Studio says. "A cup of cocoa with a marshmallow in it or a fluffy pillow is not in itself *hygge*, but it could be in the right context."

By this definition, it's likely clear that *hygge* is not an interior design style. "You cannot deliberately say something is *hygge* or design for it," Lykke confirms. Yet, it's very often thrown into décor conversations that relate to Scandinavian design. Articles like "How to *hygge* at home" or "*Hygge* style in the house" can be found across the internet, as well as stories that explain *hygge* as a fundamental element of Scandinavian decor. But go back to historical papers and articles about the Scandinavian modern movement of the 1950s and 60s and rarely, if ever, will one find a mention of the phrase.

Outside of Denmark, the term can be traced to 2016, when it was shortlisted as a word of the year by both Oxford and Collins dictionaries. The concept took over social media and publishing – dozens of books came out that year about the ideology – and was heavily used to market and sell everything from wool socks to mulled wine. "*Hygge* has been deliberately

opposite *The Gjøvik House near Oslo, Norway, was designed by Norm Architects.*

imported – and reinvented – by eager Britons," journalist Charlotte Higgins wrote in a 2016 *Guardian* article about the trend. "The concept may be indelibly Danish, but the hype has been made in London."

She posits that enthusiasm for the ideology was the result of the smart business acumen of London publishers, who called on writers to document the concept after a wildly successful – and largely random – article about *hygge* published on the BBC website in 2015. "In its most visible manifestation – the onslaught of books on the subject – it is a trend that has been carefully concocted in the laboratory of London publishing houses," she wrote.

It's fair to say that cozy, comfortable interiors are a trademark of the Scandinavian modern design aesthetic. It's also reasonable to conclude that much of the Scandinavian design philosophy is rooted in a perspective that mirrors the doctrine of *hygge*. However, from a strictly historical standpoint, *hygge* was not a part of the Scandinavian modern movement. Perhaps it was always baked into the aesthetic – after all, many of the designers would have grown up immersed in a culture that prioritized simple comfort – but the word hadn't yet voyaged outside of Denmark. "It's not something that can be used as a marketing tool, because it dilutes the concept," Lykke says.

Contemporary Scandinavian Design

S candinavian modern was the interior design look à la mode in the 1950s in the United States but lost steam over the decades as tastes and culture evolved. Movements such as postmodernism and deconstructivism pushed design in a new direction, one that was avant-garde, maximalist, eclectic and even humorous. Designers such as Ettore Sottsass (1917–2007), who founded the Memphis Group, favoured "radical, funny and outrageous" design, and rebelled against the solemnity of modern design. In the 1980s, interiors were often colourful, graphic and decadent, the near opposite of the Scandinavian ethos.

The creations of prominent Scandinavian modern designers also changed in the ensuing decades. In some cases, they moved away from the neutral wood furniture that had defined much of the movement. As technology allowed, Nordic designers experimented with materials such as plastics and fibreglass in the 1960s and 1970s. Verner Panton (1926–98) was especially interested in plastic and its ability to be moulded and shaped into seemingly endless possibilities. Conceived in 1959 but produced serially in 1967 by Vitra, he released the seminal Panton Chair, which is made from a single piece of plastic and available in bright, dazzling colours. To this day, it is still one of the most iconic pieces of furniture in design history.

Over the years, there have been moments where a mass interest in the Scandinavian modern style resurges. For example, in the 1990s an appreciation for vintage pieces surfaced, and interest in mid-century and modernist design spread again. The 2010s saw a renewed interest in the look, particularly thanks to the *hygge* craze of that time. In recent years, Scandinavian design has experienced another major resurgence. Nearly every major retailer – from budget to

boutique stores – offers "Scandinavian-inspired" furniture and pieces.

While mass retailers help keep furniture inspired by Scandinavian modernism in the minds (and hands) of the masses, contemporary Scandinavian designers continue to innovate to great success. Though the aesthetics have changed somewhat, many of these designers still create under similar beliefs: the importance of quality craftsmanship, the need for accessible products and the notion that good design improves people's lives.

Nonetheless, the historic style never fully disappeared, and likely never will. Many pieces designed by visionary creators of the 1950s and 60s are still in production, proving not only their lasting appeal, but their enduring usefulness. Perhaps this is the true reason Scandinavian design retains its status as one of the most popular design styles. After all, who doesn't want their space to be beautiful, thoughtful and, as history has proven, timeless?

previous page *A solitary wooden cottage on the Norwegian island of Vega, designed by Swedish studio Kolman Boye Architects.*

opposite *The Panton Chair, designed by Verner Panton in 1959 and mass-produced by Vitra in 1967. It was the first all-plastic chair made in one piece with a cantilever design.*

The Birth of Japandi

Though Japan and Scandinavia are vastly different historically, culturally and geographically, the two entities share notably similar principles. An interest in minimalism, functionalism and craftsmanship are among their joint design values. Additionally, both are known for serene interiors with a connection to nature. Perhaps it was only a matter of time before the two aesthetics merged.

For the average design consumer, this coalescence might seem like a new trend in the industry. Indeed, Google Trends shows that the term "Japandi" was rarely searched prior to 2019 and has noticeably grown since 2020. However, all this proves is that the portmanteau and mass interest emerged a few years ago. In reality, the history and connection between the two cultures extends all the way back to the 19th century.

opposite *The open-plan space of Kinuta Terrace, Tokyo, Japan. By Norm Architects, in collaboration with Keiji Ashizawa Design Studio and Karimoku, Japan's leading manufacturer of wooden furniture.*

"Japonisme" in Scandinavia and Other Western Nations

Beginning in 1614, the Tokugawa shogunate gradually began enacting a series of laws that controlled and severely limited trade and diplomatic relations with foreign nations. As *Encyclopedia Britannica* explains, the policy, known as *sakoku*, "largely stemmed from Japan's mistrust of foreigners". It was particularly important to the shogun to remove Christian influence, as Spain and Portugal had persistently attempted to convert Japanese citizens to their religion. By 1639, nearly every foreign nation – except for the Netherlands and China – was banned from entering Japan or trading with the country. In turn, Japanese citizens were not allowed to leave their homeland.

Over 200 years later, the United States was eager to change this. The Western power saw Japan as an important trade partner and sent Commodore Matthew C. Perry with cannon-loaded boats to the island nation, forcing an end to Japan's closed-border policy. Many changes followed due to this: the Tokugawa shogunate fell, the emperor was reinstated as the ruler of the nation, and other Western countries were able to trade with Japan once again. Most importantly in the context of Japandi design, this fostered the emergence of "Japonisme", a term that describes Western nations' increased interest in Japanese art and design, which had been a mystery for so long.

"Many people were fascinated by the Japanese way of design, both the materials they used and the simplicity of form," Dr Mirjam Gelfer-Jørgensen, an art historian and author of *Influences from Japan in Danish Art and Design 1870–2010*, says. A number of influential artists, art patrons and designers, among others, helped introduce Japanese aesthetics to Western countries. One such man was a Parisian art dealer named Siegfried Bing, who travelled to Japan in the early 1880s and assembled a large collection of Japanese art, which

was displayed at the Nordic Exhibition of Industry, Agriculture and Art in Copenhagen in 1888. Bing also published a detailed periodical called *Le Japon Artistique, Documents d'Arte et d'Industrie* (*Artistic Japan, Documents of Art and Industry*), which was available between 1888 and 1891 and contributed to the widespread appreciation of Japanese creations.

Other notable publications that contributed to "Japonisme" included Danish painter Karl Madsen's 1885 book *Japansk Malerkunst* (*Japanese Painting*), William Anderson's *The Pictorial Arts of Japan* (1886), and J. J. Rein's *The Industries of Japan* (1889). "It was a trend in many countries," Gelfer-Jørgensen says.

And of the Scandinavian nations, perhaps none had quite the profound connection with Japan as Denmark. In 2015, Designmuseum Danmark in Copenhagen opened a new exhibition titled Learning from Japan that was based on

above *A painting by George Hendrik Breitner from his Girl in Kimono series.*

Gelfer-Jørgensen's book and curated by her. The show's goal was to demonstrate how Japanese aesthetic principles influenced Danish designers, and more notably how it impacted the birth of Danish modernism. In 2017, the exhibition culminated with a celebration planned in collaboration with the Japanese embassy to celebrate 150 years of "diplomatic cooperation between Denmark and Japan".

Gelfer-Jørgensen theorizes that one of the main reasons Danish designers were so inspired by Japanese techniques was due to shared lifestyles. "People already lived very simply in Scandinavia," she says. "This must have been something that inspired Danish craftspeople to look at the Japanese, because they also lived very simply." According to her, Danish artisans were first interested in Japanese motifs, then became enthralled with Japanese treatment of materials and artistic processes.

The 2015 exhibition at Designmuseum Danmark showcased over 400 objects from Japan, as well as those that were created by Danish craftspeople inspired by Japanese design. The breadth of the objects varied in both age and influence: there were dishes from the 1800s by Danish artists decorated with Japanese nature scenes, examples of Danish silverwork inspired by Japanese bronze plant stands, and early 20th-century pottery crafted with Japanese glazing techniques, among others. It didn't always look like the "Japandi" people recognize today, but it certainly could qualify as a version of Japanese and Scandinavian harmony. "Following the book and exhibition, people were surprised to see so much had Japanese inspiration," Gelfer-Jørgensen adds.

above *A traditionally designed Japanese room.*

overleaf *The living room of Alvar Aalto's house in Helsinki, Finland, completed in 1936.*

20th-century Japandi Design

This Scandinavian interest in Japanese design had far-reaching effects, and in many ways it was a precursor to the modernist movement in the 20th century. In fact, there are a number of notable pieces from the peak of Scandinavian modernism that have a notable Japanese influence, some of which Gelfer-Jørgensen describes in her book. For example, Danish designers Børge Mogensen (1914–72) and Grethe Meyer's (1918–2008) Boligens Byggeskabe Wardrobe with sliding doors bears a striking resemblance to Japanese *fusuma* doors. Poul Kjaerholm's (1929–80) PK-111 Screen made from Oregon pine is said to have been inspired by similar ones in Japanese houses.

Indeed, a version of "Japandi" existed in the 20th century, well before the 2020s interest. Consider the residence in Rungsted Kyst, Denmark, of Halldor Gunnløgsson, a Danish architect. Though his name never received transatlantic accolades, he was an incredibly influential designer in his homeland. In his family house built in 1958, large overhanging eaves create a covered outdoor space, similar in many ways to a Japanese *engawa* (like verandas). Sliding doors were used to conceal the bedroom and kitchen and were also used to connect the garden with the home, a common feature of Japanese design. Further, a potted tree recalls *sukiya* spirit and greatly reflects the contemporary application of the Japandi aesthetic.

Of course, the Scandinavian additions are there too: historic photos show what appears to be a set of Ant chairs by Alvar Aalto pulled up to a dining table, two PK25 chairs by Poul Kjaerholm sit in a living room space, and Danish rugs dot the floors.

It's a fascinating example of the historic combination of Japanese and Scandinavian design while also representing the time in which it was created. The open floor plan firmly establishes the home's origins in the middle of the 20th century, when this style was first becoming popular. Here, spaces are delineated through fireplaces and a bookshelf, rather than walls.

Japan's influence is also visible in Alvar Aalto's family home and studio in Helsinki, Finland. Completed in 1936, Aalto designed the structure in a functionalist style, rendered in whitewashed brick and wood. The architect lived there for decades with his family, originally with his first wife, Aino Aalto (1894–1949), then his second, Elissa (1922–94). Though it was erected nearly 100 years ago, the home looks as fresh as any contemporary residence – a testament to Aalto's creative genius and the larger modern philosophy that inspired his generation of creators.

Alvar and Aino, who was also an architect and designer, crafted much of the furniture in the home, though there are touches of other Nordic visionaries, such as a pendant light by Danish designer Poul Henningsen. Nonetheless, the Scandinavian elements are inherent and self-evident.

above *The influential Boligens Byggeskabe Wardrobe, designed by Grethe Meyer and Børge Mogensen.*

overleaf *The dining room in Alvar Aalto's house.*

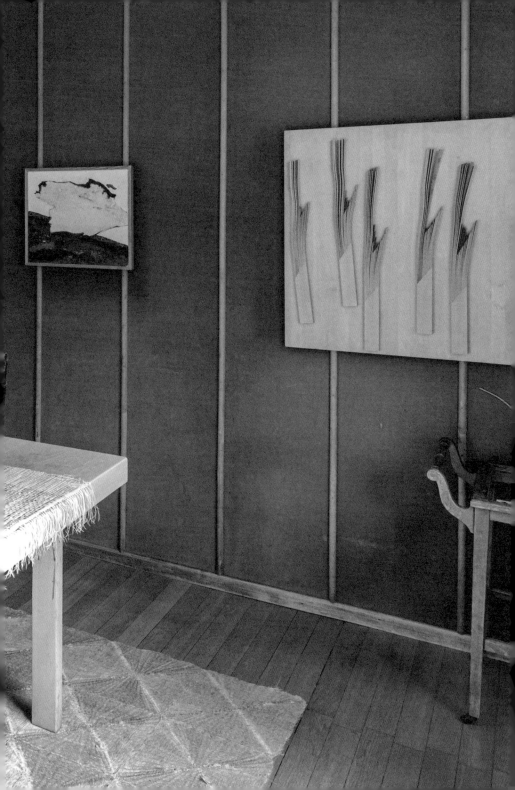

The noticeable Japanese influences, however, are worth further examination. Take the sliding door between the office and living room, a clear nod to Japanese *fusuma* doors. Like their Asian counterparts, opening and closing the door changes the layout and function of the two rooms depending on their position. A jute wall in the studio bears a resemblance to *tatami* mats, while a slat wall and weathered drink cart provides a Japanese ambiance in the dining room.

A similar convergence can be seen in Danish architect Erik Christian Sørensen's personal home in Copenhagen, completed in 1955. Here, sliding doors between the dining and living rooms create a modular floor plan, similar in many ways to traditional Japanese *shoin* and *sukiya* residences. In all of these examples, there is also a clear emphasis on natural materials, neutral colour palettes, an abundance of natural light and a connection with nature – doctrines of both Japanese and Scandinavian styles.

opposite *The hallway of Halldor Gunnløgsson's house (1958), built near the Øresund strait between Denmark and Sweden. The architecture bears a resemblance to Japanese engawa.*

above *The open-plan living area of Gunnløgsson's house.*

overleaf *The view from Gunnløgsson's bedroom, featuring minimal, practical furniture.*

Japanese design, however, was inspiring more than just Scandinavian craftspeople. Frank Lloyd Wright (1867–1959), who only admitted to three muses in his work, was heavily inspired by Japanese woodblock paintings. Walter Gropius (1883–1969), a German-American architect and founder of the Bauhaus school, was also inspired by the country's design. In 1954, he visited Japan for three months and wrote a piece about his experience in *Perspecta*, the Yale architectural journal. According to the essay, he believed Japanese architecture had already "found the answer to many of our modern requirements of simplicity, of outdoor-indoor relations, of modular coordination, and at the same time variety of expression, resulting in a common form language uniting all individual efforts."

Elizabeth Gordon

While modern designers in Europe and America were drawing inspiration from Japan, Elizabeth Gordon (1906–2000), a legendary design editor who helmed *House Beautiful* from 1939 until 1964, was spreading the word about both Scandinavian and Japanese design. Born in 1906 in Logansport, Indiana, she briefly taught in Wisconsin before moving to New York City in the 1930s and working her way into the editorial world.

In her leadership position at *House Beautiful*, she believed it was her role to educate Americans on "good" design – or rather, what she thought was "good" design. In fact, in a biographical memo she described the publication, saying, "I used *House Beautiful* as a propaganda and teaching tool – to broaden people's 'thinking-and-wanting' apparatus."

Nothing exemplifies this quite like the essay she published in 1953 titled "The Threat to the Next America". In the article, Gordon essentially argued that designers such as Walter Gropius, Ludwig Mies van der Rohe and Le Corbusier were steering the country towards communism through visual severity and "unliveable" homes. The essay was controversial and sparked opposition, but it also gained her allies, most notably Frank Lloyd Wright.

According to Gordon, there was a difference between "good" and "bad" modern. "Good" modern created homes that were both beautiful to look at and comfortable to live in. This should not be confused with what she described as a "clinical look" modern, which she felt was a bad part of the larger modern movement.

Though her critique of a European-born style might imply a nationalist bias, Gordon was not against cultural exchange. Indeed, she was a staunch supporter of two foreign design frameworks: Scandinavian and Japanese. In fact, many trace the idea for the 1954 exhibition Design in Scandinavia to Gordon.

In the February 1954 edition of the magazine, she wrote about the exhibit, saying, "When I first saw the furniture, ceramics and needlework of Scandinavia, I was literally overwhelmed by what I saw." This excerpt came not just from a report of the show, but in an editorialized article titled "Why the new Scandinavian show is important to America". She finished with the implication that the style of design was worthy of her approval because it was focused on people and democracy. "Aimed at Scandinavian home life, their designs have a natural beauty and usefulness for our own, for we are both deeply democratic people. Home is their centre – and people are the centre of their homes." In 1972, the editor reaffirmed her support for the style when she published a special issue on Scandinavian design, which was so successful she was awarded a Finnish knighthood.

Notably, she also played a key role in promoting Japanese design to consumers. In 1959, she travelled to Japan with three *House Beautiful* staffers, where she learned the term

shibui, which loosely translates to a subtle and understated form of beauty. She was so enamoured with what she discovered during her time in the country that she returned twice more.

In August and September of 1960, these research trips resulted in two back-to-back issues of *House Beautiful* about *shibui* and Japanese design (the second was about how to use American products to channel a *shibui* spirit). According to the National Museum of Asian Art Archives, the August issue was so wildly popular that after it sold out, resellers offered it to buyers for $10 – 20 times more than the 50 cents it was sold for on newsstands. The issues are often credited with introducing Japanese design to the American public and inspired a travelling exhibition based on the magazines, which toured 11 museums between 1961 and 1964.

Of course, given the similarities between Japanese styles and Scandinavian modern ones, it's not surprising that she was drawn to both. Gordon passed away in 2000, but the mass interest in Japandi shows her lasting leadership. "She was an amazingly influential editor, crusading for the softer side of contemporary design," Louis Oliver Gropp, the editor-in-chief of *House Beautiful* from 1991 until 2000, told *The New York Times* in an obituary for Gordon. "When she covered a topic, she did it in staggering depth."

previous page *Elizabeth Gordon, circa 1949.*

right *Plants bring vibrancy to a living room and dining area in an otherwise neutral home.*

Japandi Design Today

Today, "Japandi" describes the design style used to denote interiors that include both traditional and contemporary Japanese and Scandinavian aesthetics. It can be thought of as a fusion of the function and coziness of Scandinavian design with the cooler, sometimes rougher tones of Japanese design. And it is wildly popular: it's common to find interiors in the style printed on glossy magazine pages, retailers now sell "Japandi-inspired" pieces, and consumers search the phrase thousands of times per month.

Some mark the 2020 pandemic as the catalyst for the style's stratospheric growth. Most people spent their days at home and desired a place that offered peace during an era filled with uncertainty. Minimal spaces that were still comfortable and warm offered a cocoon-like embrace, and the style's emphasis on nature offered serenity when the outside world felt nothing but tumultuous. Given the spike in popularity in 2020, there's certainly evidence to support this.

However, as history shows, this is not the first time aesthetics from the two cultures have merged. "The bond goes much deeper," says Lykke. OEO Studio also has project offices in Tokyo and has developed its design ethos around both Nordic and Japanese values. "Each has an appreciation for simplicity, quality and craftsmanship. It's a part of the DNA of both."

In fact, Lykke isn't the biggest fan of the word "Japandi", because he feels it can imply a fleeting trend, which is ultimately a disservice to Japanese design, Scandinavian design, and any convergence of the two. "My concern is when people start putting something in a box and calling it 'Japandi'," he explains. There are a number of instances where the term is used as a marketing tool to commodify and profit from, which "exploits the cultures and oftentimes leads to diluted quality," he adds. "Karl Lagerfeld said 'trendy is the last stage before tacky', so I

opposite *A minimalist living room, with warmth from the artificial fire and softness introduced by the plant.*

don't want it to be a trend, because that's not fair."

While there is certainly increased attention on the design style now dubbed "Japandi", nothing proves its staying power quite like the centuries worth of intertwined history. "In a lot of the great architects and design masters of the past, you can see there was a lot of inspiration," Lykke says. Some, like Halldor Gunnløgsson's home, look in many ways like the Japandi aesthetic many recognize today. Others, like the pottery of late 1800s and early 1900s, exemplify the connection in a different way. In either case, the relationship is there.

However, it's not always even necessary to go that far back. Look in interior magazines from the mid-2010s, and it isn't hard to find projects with a distinct Japanese and Scandinavian flare. Perhaps this was because the *hygge* craze of 2016 was occurring nearly in tandem with the rising popularity of Marie Kondo's decluttering doctrine (*The Life-Changing Magic of Tidying Up* was originally published in English in late 2014). Consumers were flooded with information about Danish and Japanese culture – both of which were presented to offer happier, calmer and cozier lives – and unsurprisingly people began combining them. Some design publications from the time even referred to the look with a different portmanteau: Japanordic.

In short, the connection between Japanese and Scandinavian design has looked different over the years, but it has been present for nearly 200. As Lykke explains, people can and will continue to interpret "Japandi" differently over the years, but the connection will not disappear. After all, "both cultures value design that can stand the test of time," he says.

"We think a lot about the experience we want to create in our design and how we want people to feel in the space," says Lykke of OEO Studio's work. "It's not just one individual thing, it's the wholeness of the project and how everything works together." The following pages showcase exceptional designs from OEO, Norm Architects, and more that embody Japandi style—not just in one aspect of the room but in all elements of the composition, from the use of light and shadow, to material palettes and indoor-outdoor transitions.

These incredible examples also demonstrate that there is no one way to pull off a Japandi room—they can be minimal

showrooms

and reserved, bold and rich, or somewhere in the middle. Much of it comes down to the various creative ways designers interpret traditional and historical motifs and reimagine them in a contemporary setting. In a villa near the Great Wall of China designed by Kengo Kuma, tatami mats and a floor mattress appear in a very straightforward reference to traditional Japanese design. In a Yekaterinburg, Russia, apartment, the Japanese influence is seen more subtly through the use of an open floor plan, while Hans Wegner's fashionable CH20 Elbow Chairs create a distinct link to Scandinavian modernism. Both—and every other project highlighted—are successful for unique and singular reasons.

In this chapter, discover a collection of striking Japandi rooms and uncover the compelling reasons they work so well.

previous page *Japandi homes
are minimal, streamlined, and
highlight natural materials, as
demonstrated in this Copenhagen
home by Norm Architects.
The recessed shelving draws
inspiration from Japanese*
tokonoma *and* chigai-dana, *and
the staggered decor pulls from the
Japanese tradition of asymmetry.
Smooth light wood on the shelves
and floors is reminiscent of
Scandinavian furniture while the
organic grey walls offer a nod to
textured mud walls in Japanese
tea rooms.*

left *Materiality is decoration in
this Tokyo residence, designed as a
collaboration between
Copenhagen-based Norm
Architects and Tokyo-based studio
Keiji Ashizawa. From the textured
walls to the wood grain on the
table, there is little need for
additional ornamentation. The
potted tree brings color into the
room and adds organic lines to the
otherwise geometric composition.*

left *A bedroom in central Tokyo, designed by OEO Studio in collaboration with developer ReBITA/R100 TOKYO. Curtains diffuse soft light throughout the space reminiscent of shoji screens. Cream and white accents seen in the bedding and lamp shades complement the dark bed frame, room divider, and floor lamp.*

left *It can be challenging to create visual interest when working primarily with simple, clean lines and neutral color palettes. Designers often combat this by infusing an abundance of texture into projects, as seen in this entryway designed by OEO Studio with ReBITA/R100 TOKYO. Glossy tiles juxtapose next to a coarse rug while wood contrasts the light brown wall covering. Elevation changes in the floor and the tray ceiling add further dimension.*

overleaf *Accent furniture can be a compelling way to create a focal point in a room, as seen in this project by Montreal-based Talo Studios. Located on the southern side of Mount Royal, the Hans Wegner Flag Halyard Chair directly next to a well-weathered potted tree embodies the Japandi spirit perfectly. Talo Studios founder, Tiina Vahtola, removed a wall between the kitchen and living room to add more light and permanence to the room. Before the renovation, "the living room felt like a small, dark and forgotten space," Vahtola told Dezeen.*

opposite and above *Nature is art in this cabin nestled deep in the Swedish mountains, designed by Tina Bergman Architects. Named the Hat House, the windows frame the birch trees in the forest beyond, offering an ever-changing picture as the seasons turn. Furnishings are minimal and functional so as not to pull focus from the beauty just beyond the glass partition. A built-in window seat offers further connection to the exterior, an important philosophy in both Japanese and Scandinavian traditions. The all-over spruce paneling could recall traditional Finnish saunas, though the design motif speaks more to the home's perfect harmony with its surroundings.*

previous pages *This Los Angeles home incorporates a number of contemporary interpretations of Japanese interior motifs – most notably, a nature scene on the closet door reminiscent of traditional Japanese painted screens, called byōbu. Crafted by Shanty Wijaya of ALLPRACE, the designer creatively used a paper fan as decor while multiple doors with expansive windows provide connection to the outdoors. "The lifestyle that [Japanese and Scandinavian] design styles aim for is more about creating a space that is functional and artistic. That's why it feels homey, and it's not too stark or sterile," Wijaya told Coveteur in 2021 about the project.*

A mossy green accent wall defines the living room in this Yekaterinburg, Russia apartment designed by URAL, a Moscow-based studio. The open floor plan creates an airy and relaxed atmosphere while modern furnishings, such as Hans Wegner's CH20 Elbow Chairs add Scandinavian flair, and the couch's low profile and simple silhouette recalls traditional Japanese furnishings.

left *Though Japandi interiors are often minimal, this doesn't mean they must be sterile. Creating comfortable, cozy environments is an extremely important part of the style and was often a priority for modernist Scandinavian designers. A wall-mounted fireplace is the crowning feature of this living room, though soft furnishing and indirect lighting add to the warm and homey ease.*

previous page *Green is among the most popular accent colors in Japandi design and is often integrated in the space through indoor plants or artwork. This kitchen explores another medium to introduce the verdant hue: marble. The choice honors Japandi's inclination towards natural materials, but does so in an exciting and unique way. Using wood slats as an accent on the ceilings, walls, and cabinetry adds even more visual interest while maintaining a neutral and sophisticated feel. A number of finishing touches such as the modernist chairs and barstools, textured bowls, and an oversized paper lantern infuse elements of both Scandinavian and Japanese design while pulling the whole room together.*

right *Originally conceived as a private collection of villas by 12 leading Asian architects, this residence was designed by Kengo Kuma. Called Great (Bamboo) Wall, the retreat is located in the Shuiguan Mountains and was completed in 2002. The main bedroom, seen here, showcases how traditional Japanese furnishings can still function in a contemporary setting. The bed is directly on the ground, similar to shikibuton (Japanese futon mattresses designed to be placed on the floor). Tatami mats cover a portion of the room, though wood flooring still peaks out as a reminder of the union between the traditional and contemporary.*

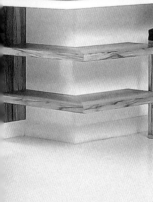

previous page *Opting for streamlined, unfussy furniture is among the simplest ways to achieve the Japandi look, as seen in this living room. The furnishings in the room highlight geometric shapes, such as the rectangular silhouette and cylindrical pillow on the Barcelona Day Bed by Ludwig Mies Van Der Rohe, the circular tabletop, or the half-oval console table. Additionally, most of the decor is both functional and beautiful, such as the candles or throw blanket.*

right *Traditional Japanese homes were built with wood, and many Scandinavian modern designers were revered for the innovative manner they manipulated and shaped the material when crafting furniture. Naturally, finding creative ways to introduce wood into a space is a compelling strategy when designing a Japandi room. This kitchen does this exceptionally well, from standard inclusions in the dining table and chairs to wood paneling on the appliances. Large doors that can easily open and connect the room to the exterior emphasize the contemporary style's penchant for harmony with nature.*

left *There is very little excess in this dining room: the only decorative additions are a book, a bowl of fruit, and a vase with sparse stems. The table – characterized by its minimal profile and clean lines – defines most of the room and notably draws inspiration from the sleek wooden furniture designed during the peak of the Scandinavian modern movement. Though wood remains the most prominent material in the room, natural fibers seen in the window treatments and chair cushions soften the space while maintaining a sense of organic flow. Additionally, a number of traditional Japanese motifs are reinterpreted throughout the room, such as a recessed alcove with open shelving, similar to* tokonoma *and* chigai-dana, *and the branches, offering a nod to* ikebana *arrangements.*

right *Blurring the boundaries between the interior and exterior was among the primary goals for Norm Architects when working on this seaside home in Denmark. To achieve this, the firm relied on "sensuous, natural elements" throughout the interiors, as seen in the tapestry, woven basket, and linens in the bedroom. The color palette mirrors the natural landscape, drawing inspiration from moody coastal skies, soft sand coloring, and the wispy browns of the grass banks. "Boasting all-natural, rich materials, the house gives you the feeling of being in the middle of nature while inside," the firm said in a statement to Dezeen.*

overleaf *Statement lighting in this Japandi kitchen adds movement and interest to the space while maintaining an overall simple and streamlined look. Further, the room models how designers can play with balance to blend Scandi and Japanese philosophies. Symmetry, seen in the island and bar stools, could be interpreted as more Scandinavian-leaning, as much of the furniture that was designed during the era was even and uniform. Japanese aesthetics and architecture, on the other hand, have historically favored asymmetry, representing the lack of perfection in nature. The artfully uneven cabinetry and open shelving brings this point of view into the design.*

next page *New York City-based firm Cicognani Kalla Architect designed this artist's studio in Greenwich Village, New York City, USA. Painted brick and ceiling beams introduce texture to the room, which is bathed in light thanks to floor-to-ceiling windows. The low-profile furniture is reminiscent of traditional Japanese furnishings, while all decor is thoughtfully curated. A Japanese room divider complements modernist furnishings, such as the floor lamp.*

above *Despite the relatively small footprint of this vignette, the space is made complete with multiple colors and textures, from the cool-toned, grey-washed stairs to the chair's woven seat and back. The sharp angles of Pierre Jeanneret's Kangaroo Chair mirror the architecture of the stairwell and demonstrate how functional items, such as a seat, can serve as sculpture in Japandi-style homes.*

opposite *In traditional Japanese aesthetics, "Ma" refers to the idea that unused area is equally as important as filled space. This Japandi-inspired living room makes use of this notion exceptionally well through the bookshelf's artful curation. Ample negative space makes the room appear more relaxed and provides breathing room to admire each bowl, vase, or plate. Streamlined furniture and earthy tones round out the room.*

Among the many popular contemporary design styles, Japandi is perhaps one of the easiest to replicate. Unlike some aesthetics such as maximalism – which, by definition, involves significant collecting – Japandi asks for paring down. Indeed, the first step for anyone looking to implement the Japandi look into their home should likely be decluttering.

Wabi-sabi reminds designers to appreciate the beauty in simple and imperfect things. This means, instead of reaching for a catalogue to source a brand-new couch or coffee table, it can be worth repurposing – and even falling back in love with – items you already own. In short, by purging unnecessary items and honouring the history of what stays, you're already halfway to a Japandi home.

For those eager to bring the vision across the finish line, this section covers specific design elements and practical

elements

advice for recreating the look in any home. From colour and material palettes to furniture and décor, the Japandi look may only be a few small changes away.

opposite *An inviting view through a circular window into Mike Belleme's cabin in Swannanoa, North Carolina, USA – a small but perfectly formed blend of Japanese and Scandinavian design.*

Start With a Minimal Base

Japandi interiors are defined by their rustic and relaxed simplicity. Both Japanese and Scandinavian design principles focus on functionalism over excess, so it's important to start with a clean and minimal base.

Pare Down Your Furniture

This doesn't mean you should donate everything except a bed and a single chair, but take time to consider what you *truly* need in your home. Is your couch big enough that you can do away with that recliner? Is the top of your desk collecting dust while the drawers collect junk because you do all of your work from the kitchen table? Maybe it's time to ditch it. Focus on what will make the house as functional as possible for the occupants, and cut the rest.

Smart Storage

Storage can be a game-changer when it comes to nailing the Japandi look. Opt for furniture such as chests, wardrobes, cabinets or credenzas with plenty of space. Tuck away all the odds and ends that may be necessary to your happiness in the home – like remotes, board games or clothes – but that don't need to be on display at all times.

Take Your Time When Decorating

The joy that comes from putting together a dream home can be thrilling, but slowing down ensures you're intentional with decisions and basing them on genuine needs. You may think you want a bigger dining room table, then realize that you rarely host more than a few friends, and that space – and budget – may be better allocated towards something else.

Invest in Fewer, High-quality Items

Both Japanese and Scandinavian design prioritize well-made and sturdy pieces. Instead of buying ten new items that may not last more than a few years, invest in one quality piece at a time. Not only will the piece serve you better, the outcome will look more polished.

Remember the Wow Factor

Minimal interiors still need focal points. Consider where – and what – you want to draw attention to. Perhaps it's one striking piece of art or a unique statement chair; just make sure there is a wow moment.

above *A custom window bench and built-in storage in a Montreal home by Talo Studios, Canada.*

Neutral and Earthy Colour Palette

The colour palette in most Japandi designs is neutral, though this doesn't mean the spaces are all white. Hues often draw inspiration from nature and highlight colours such as brown, cream, green and grey. Other colours, such as light pinks, warm yellows and terracotta oranges also make appearances. Generally, hues are muted and matte, but there is no one way to nail the Japandi chromas.

White and Browns

Contrasting white and brown is a common technique in Japandi interiors. Often, brown is introduced through wood furniture while white appears on walls and soft furnishings. This palette can work well in rooms that already benefit from an abundance of natural light, as the rays will contribute to an overall relaxed and airy mood.

Greys and Black

Moodier Japandi rooms may feature neutral shades on the darker end of the colour spectrum, such as greys and blacks. Some even refer to the look as "dark Japandi". This application can be especially useful in projects with multiple rooms designed in the style. Not only will it break up repetition but can also aid in creating dimension between various spaces. Consider painting walls a slate grey and furnish with darker woods and black furniture.

Adding Pops of Colour

When designing your project, look for ways to introduce colour into the room, as vibrancy will add life to the space. Art, plants, pillows, blankets, vases and rugs are all potential vessels to bring chroma into the design. It's common to see pops of green in Japandi interiors, whether in paint, furniture or through plants. However, other colours can be fair game, too. For a statement, infusing an unexpected colour, such as a bright pink, can be extremely impactful.

opposite *A neutral dining area in the Azabu Residence, Tokyo, Japan. Designed by Norm Architects, in collaboration with Keiji Ashizawa Design and Japanese furniture brand Karimoku Case.*

Let There Be Light

Windows are among the most crucial elements to successfully pulling off a Japandi design. Not only do they inspire indoor-outdoor living – a common feature in both Japanese and Scandinavian design – but contribute to the overall atmosphere of the room, whatever the weather. On sunny days, the rays add warmth to the space while views of dreary skies only make snuggles on the couch that much cozier.

Framing Windows

Shakkei, which translates to "borrowed scenery", is a concept that originates in China, though it is most often associated with Japanese garden design. Traditionally, it refers to the practice of incorporating a distant landscape – such as a mountain, hill or waterfall – into the garden design. In a modern setting, this could mean framing specific vistas – or, if this is not possible, using the available view as "art" in the room.

Circular Windows

In Japanese, round windows are called *Marumado*. The soothing shape is a particularly common motif in Japanese architecture. Genko-an temple in Kyoto holds one of the most notable circular windows, called the window of Satori, or the window of spiritual awakening or enlightenment. Drawing inspiration from the Zen ensō, a round window can add a quintessential Japanese aesthetic to a home.

Floor-to-ceiling Windows

A number of structural innovations in the 20th century resulted in the emergence of glass curtain walls – that is, non-load-bearing exteriors that simply enclosed the building. Not only does this offer a seamless indoor-outdoor connection, but it carries a modernist connotation that's useful when crafting a Japandi home. Sliding *fusuma* doors leading to a garden offer a similar effect, promoting an uninterrupted connection between outside and in.

opposite *A floor-to-ceiling window lets light flood in and brings out the warm tones in natural materials.*

Contemporary Interpretations of Traditional Designs

Reimagining elements of traditional Japanese design in a contemporary way is a great way to honour the legacy of the aesthetic's origins. Bonus points if you use Scandinavian-leaning details – like light wood – in this rethinking. The following ideas showcase innovative ways to pull this off.

Translucent Curtains

Translucent curtains that softly disperse light can be an innovative way to subtly reference *shoji* screens. The soft treatments can also foster a cozy mood in the room.

opposite and above *Dark wood and discreet, built-in furniture help make these spaces practical as well as beautiful. Designed by Norm Architects, in collaboration with Keiji Ashizawa Design and Japanese furniture brand Karimoku Case.*

Alcoves

To recall the *tokonoma* seen in *shoin* residences, consider crafting an alcove to display artwork, pictures or other decorative objects, like this one by Norm Architects.

Shelves, however, mustn't be restricted to just alcoves. Any open shelving can be viewed as an interpretation of the Japanese *chigai-dana*. Ideally, open shelves would be implemented for both function and beauty, so consider displaying objects, such as bowls or vases, that do the same.

Built-in Furniture

Another notable design feature that emerged in *shoin* architecture is the *tsuke-shoin*, featuring a built-in desk alcove. This same sentiment can be put to work in a modern Japandi home. In addition to desks, consider built-in benches, wardrobes or tables.

Statement Ceilings

Ceilings in traditional Japanese design were often given great care, such as the coffered ones in *shoin* buildings. Painting the ceiling a unique colour and adding beams are two popular ways designers add interest.

Tatami Mats

Woven rugs made from jute, seagrass, sisal linen or similar materials can allude to traditional Japanese *tatami* mats. However, these fibres don't have to be just used on the floor, they could also appear on furniture or as wall art.

opposite *Recessed shelving with decorative objects in Heatherhill Beach House by Norm Architects, Vejby, Denmark.*

Texture is Everything

Japandi interiors are relatively subdued, and texture is among the primary ways designers create visual interest in the compositions. Often, incorporating a variety of textures is key to pulling off the look.

Natural Materials

The use of natural materials is often described as a core element of the Japandi aesthetic. This is particularly useful, not just to honour two cultures that have traditionally prioritized handicrafts and manmade construction, but also because it ensures a variety of texture. Consider the difference between linen and cotton, stone and wood, rattan and leather. When used collectively, the varying appearance and feel of the materials add depth and character to the home. Further, the simplicity of organic objects contributes to a laid-back and effortless look.

Juxtaposition

Japandi interiors are particularly successful when there is a deliberate juxtaposition between textures: for example, the waxy, glossy finish of a plant potted in a rough and rustic vase or a thin paper lantern near a sturdy kitchen table.

Slats

Slats and wall panelling are other common tools used to create dimension in Japandi rooms. It's common to see this technique used to define an accent wall, though it may also be used on furniture, as a room divider or even on the ceiling. Moreover, the detail recalls Japanese *sudare* (screens or blinds).

above left *Textured throw cushions are an easy and inexpensive way to add texture to living spaces.*

above right *Panelling on the ceiling of this kitchen adds warmth and coziness, as well as highlighting the natural beauty of the wood.*

Wabi-sabi

Japandi homes generally honour the *wabi-sabi* philosophy. This can be achieved in a number of ways, from the simple appreciation of the objects you already own, to deliberate aesthetic decisions. Below are several ways to infuse a *wabi-sabi* modus operandi.

Limewash

Limewash paint, made from crushed limestone, water and pigments, is known for its chalky, textured appearance. When used, the colouring results in a worn-in finish, perfect for a Japandi home. It's common to see Japandi interiors with grey and cream walls, though nothing is off limits.

Rough Wood

To easily add a rustic and humble touch to a room, consider sourcing furniture, shelves or finishes made from rough wood. Things like bark, knots, discoloration or spalting all add depth to the branch while reminding observers of the earth's endless supply of organic beauty.

Textured Objects

Given its roots in the Japanese tea ceremony, the objects that originally embodied the *wabi-sabi* philosophy were often bowls and cups, which historians describe as simple and proudly weathered. Today, consider incorporating textured vases, pots or similar objects to convey that homespun purity in a contemporary way.

opposite *Limewashing walls in a minimalist bedroom adds texture and a lived-in feel.*

opposite *Unfinished wood provides visual and tactile interest, introducing the natural world into an interior space.*

above *Texture in this living space makes it an inviting, comfortable space with only a few select objects and finishes.*

Iconic Furniture

Because there are so many pieces of iconic Scandinavian modern furniture, incorporating these designs – or ones inspired by them – goes a long way when crafting a Japandi home. Leggy chairs, light wood and simple silhouettes are all hallmark traits of Scandinavian pieces, though there is variety and these features aren't essential to the aesthetic.

Chairs

Many Scandinavian designers were known for their chair designs. Whether accents, dining, desk or otherwise, adding Scandinavian seating to a room is a frequent element of Japandi rooms. Hans Wegner's Wishbone Chair, seen here, is a quintessential piece from the era and adds an instant touch of Danish modern.

Lighting

Lamps and light fixtures were another area where Scandinavian designers innovated greatly. Like chairs, functionality was paramount, and many pieces from the era featured clean lines, simple compositions and natural materials. Poul Henningsen, more commonly known by his initials P. H., is perhaps the most famous Danish lighting designer, known for pioneering a three-shade light system that eliminated harsh glares by softly diffusing light.

Rugs

Though bright colours aren't often associated with the Japandi style, there are still ways to introduce chroma into a home. One of the most authentic ways to do this could be through rugs, particularly Finnish ones. Known as a *ryijy*, these long-tufted runners date back hundreds of years in the Nordic nation and are characterized by their innovative use of colour and pattern. Loja Saarinen, a Finnish-American textile artist, is particularly celebrated for the rugs that she and her studio created.

opposite *The iconic wishbone chairs of Hans Wegner.*

Contemporary Furniture

opposite *Clean lines and sleek, furniture and units keep this modern kitchen bright.*

Of course, most Japandi homes aren't furnished exclusively with vintage Scandinavian pieces. Not only might this fail to address the Japanese half of the design style, but it might not capture the contemporary influence that is also present in Japandi homes. When sourcing pieces, consider the following.

Clean Lines

Look for furniture with clean, smooth, crisp lines. As previously mentioned, natural materials are paramount to the look, so source pieces made from wood, leather, rattan or similar materials. Couches are usually devoid of prints and instead feature a single neutral colour, such as white, cream or beige.

Low Profiles

Low-profile furniture is currently popular across a number of interior design styles. Many contemporary couches and beds are mere inches off of the ground, but the look dates back hundreds of years. Consider a *chabudai,* a type of Japanese table. These were intentionally designed low to the ground so diners could sit on the floor while eating. Or the traditional Japanese *shikibuton,* which is a hand-quilted mattress that is placed directly on *tatami* mats. For a Japandi home, it may be worth including a few contemporary low-profile pieces inspired by this history.

Paper Lanterns

Paper lanterns are another common addition to Japandi homes. Isamu Noguchi, a Japanese-American artist and landscape architect, was celebrated for his Akari Light Sculptures, which were crafted following a traditional Japanese method. Incorporating a paper lantern, whether a Noguchi or otherwise, is a flattering addition to almost any Japandi room.

above *This bedroom puts texture at the forefront, with choice pops of colour and discreet built-in furniture.*

opposite *A paper lantern brings softness and warm light to a space, as seen here in this dining room designed by American design firm Bespoke Only.*

Functional Décor

Since Japandi interiors are characterized by their minimalist aesthetic, it is less common to find décor just for décor's sake. Instead, decoration is achieved through objects that are beautiful, but more importantly functional. Think about the products you use every day – from coffee makers to hand towels – and the ways they can contribute to the overall design of the space.

Plates, Bowls and Cups

Sourcing handmade dinnerware with "imperfections" is a particularly successful way to transmit a *wabi-sabi* aesthetic. Consider placing a large bowl on the counter or dining table or styling dishes on an open shelf to pull out when necessary.

Vases

Like dishware, vases with visible texture and a worn patina are often favoured over others with smooth or glossy finishes. Display flowers, branches or other plants to bring life into the home.

Benches

Benches are infinitely useful, which is perhaps why they're such frequent additions in Japandi homes. The ideal place to lace up shoes or pack a bag on your way out of the door, a bench serves both a purpose and is often the perfect aesthetic touch in hallways, on the ends of beds or in mudrooms.

Storage

As noted at the beginning of this chapter, furniture with plenty of storage is key in a Japandi home. When planning your space, take care when selecting wardrobes, shelves, chests, armoires or similar pieces. In addition to being places to store all of your goods, think about them as defining elements of the design.

opposite *A practical and beautiful block of wood serves as a bench in this beachfront house by Norm Architects.*

Flowers, Plants and Trees

In addition to functional décor, plants and flowers are often used in Japandi homes to further establish the organic nature of the look. However, they're often used sparingly: a vase displaying a few branches on a coffee table or a single potted tree in a corner are common applications.

Branches

Decorating with branches is particularly useful in a Japandi room, as it brings to mind a connection to wood that both the Scandinavian and Japanese design cultures embrace. Further, it's a subtle way to reference *sukiya* architecture, which often employed wood in the design with the bark still attached.

There are multiple ways to incorporate branches into a space, but it's common to see them in vases on coffee tables, counters or even kitchen tables. In general, these should be used sparingly. Think of their natural contours and bends as a way to add delicate contrast between the clean, straight lines of the rest of the design.

Live Stems

You may not frequently find a bouquet of red roses or yellow tulips in a Japandi design, but that doesn't mean live flowers can't be a part of the look. If striving to add colour to the space through florals, consider an *ikebana* arrangement, which is often less dense than a Western design and prioritizes asymmetry and negative space.

Trees

Extend the indoor-outdoor connection celebrated in the Japandi style by bringing trees into the home. From bonsai to potted trees, there are a number of ways to pull this off successfully. When selecting trees for your project, consider what growing conditions they require in addition to the amount of space available for them. For homes that can welcome more substantial greenery, consider potted trees such as a ficus, mini olive tree, Japanese maple or weeping fig.

opposite *Blossoming cherry branches in handmade clay vases.*

above *A simple plant is made into a statement piece by its placement on a simple pedestal.*

opposite *A sliding door in the Azabu Residence in Tokyo, Japan, by Norm Architects allows for open-plan or divided spaces, with foliage to soften the space.*

Finding Balance

No rule in Japandi design says a space must be equal parts Japanese and Scandinavian. In fact, it's quite common to see rooms that lean more one way or another, even in the same house. When designing your space, consider how much of each style you want present. Of course, there is no right answer, but taking the time to properly consider the balance will result in a more successful application.

opposite *A statement-making staircase in a Japandi-inspired home.*

More Scandinavian?
For a more Scandinavian design, opt for lighter colours in the design. White or cream walls; furniture made from beech, pine, ash or oak; and textural elements such as sheepskin rugs or chunky throw blankets could all contribute to this.

The more Nordic-heavy look might make sense in homes located in colder climates that could benefit from the cozy quality of Scandinavian design. With that in mind, this tactic can also be effective in rooms with big fireplaces or those you plan to curl up in, such as a reading or family room.

Or, More Japanese?
To achieve a more Japanese-influenced space, consider using dark or medium-toned woods, such as ebony. Reclaimed hand-hewn timber is especially applicable. Integrating modern *shoji* screens, movable room dividers and *tatami* mats can increase the Japanese feel.

Non-negotiables
Of course, no matter which Japanese-Scandinavian split you choose to implement, remember the similarities of both design aesthetics: natural light, a minimalist profile, a functional emphasis and quality craftsmanship. Since both cultures prioritize them, think of them as non-negotiables. Start here, and the Japandi look is well within anyone's grasp.

Index

ACKNOWLEDGEMENTS

A big thank you to my parents and Anna for all of their love and support;
the historians and designers who were kind enough to share their time and expertise with me;
and Heather Boisseau, Matt Tomlinson, and everyone else at OH/Headline who helped make this book possible.

PICTURE CREDITS

The publishers would like to thank the following for their kind permission to reproduce the images in this book.

Cover images: © Jonas Bjerre-Poulsen, courtesy of Norm Architects (front); © iStock, FollowTheFlow (back)

Alamy Phillip Harrington 45; Viktoriia Kovalchuk 114–5. **Allprace Homes** Alex Zarour 96–7, 129 (architecture and design by Shanty Wijaya of Allprace Homes). **Atelier Bejee** B. Hommes and M. Briones 100. **Bespoke Only** John Daniel 147. **Bridgeman** Iberforto 18–9. **Carl Hansen** 35, 143, 158. **CUBO Design Architects** Koichi Torimura 29 (architectural design by Hitoshi Saruta). **Flickr** Benh Lieu Song 9; janwillemsen 47l; Ninara 64–5, 68–9. **Fritz Hansen** 39, 49. **Georg Jensen** 49. **Getty** Bettmann 43; Caia Image 146; DEA/W. BUSS 16; Eric Lafforgue/Art in All of Us 74; Heritage Images 61; Historical Picture Archive 21; Housewife/Stringer 34; John S Lander 25; Kamal Zharif bin Kamaludin 63; Pictures from History 23; REDA&CO 151; Tsuneo Yamashita 13; Werner Forman 27; Zhang Peng 15. **Gubi** 42. **Heyday Möbel** 67. **Hiroto Kawaguch** 30–1 (design by Kawaguch, photography by Yosuke Ohtake). **Huntington Library** Maynard L. Parker, courtesy of The Huntington Library, San Marino, California, 77. **Interior Archive** Annie Schlechter 144 (design by Joe Serrins); Patrick van Robaeys/Basset-Images 140 (design by Stephanie Boiteux Gallard); Simon Upton 104–5 (architecture by Kengo Kuma). **iStock** brizmaker 128; FollowTheFlow 79; Hoxton/Tom Merton 135; Mesamong 13. **Kolman Boyle Architects** 55 (photography by Ake Eson Lindman). **Mike Belleme** 121. **Norm Architects** 2, 4–5, 51, 52, 59, 82, 85, 86, 113, 125, 130, 131, 132, 149, 152, 153. **OEO Studio** Aoki Michinori 136–7; Michinori Aoki 88–9, 90–1. **OTTO** Francesco Lagnese 116–7 (designed by Beatrice Caracciolo). **Realdania By & Byg** Anders Sune Berg 75; Jakob Bekker-Hansen 70, 71, 72–3. **Talo Studio** Brooke Stephenson/Found My Thrill 92–3, 123. **Tina Bergman Architects** Jim Stephenson 94–5. UME Architecture David Chatfield 102–3. **Unsplash** Don Kaveen 108; Jason Briscoe 154; Maria Orlova 139; Tina Witherspoon 134; Zhao Yangyang 7, 81, 106–7, 110, 118, 119, 127, 141. **Ural Interiors** 98–9. **Wikimedia Commons** Soramimi 10; Brooklyn Museum 33; Daderot 41, 44; EW3234 38; SteinsplitterBot 24; TheGoodEndedHappily 37, 57.

Special thanks to Norm Architects (normcph.com) for the use of their images, including the cover image.

opposite *A Japandi inspired dining room creates a calm and serene atmosphere.*

Cover images: ©Jonas Bjerre-Poulsen/Norm Architects (front); ©iStock/FollowTheFlow (back)

First published in 2025 by OH
An Imprint of HEADLINE PUBLISHING GROUP LIMITED

1

Cataloguing in Publication Data is available from the British Library

Hardback ISBN 978-1-83861-220-7

Printed and bound in China

Headline's policy is to use papers that are natural, renewable and recyclable products
and made from wood grown in well-managed forests and other controlled sources.
The logging and manufacturing processes are expected to conform to the environmental
regulations of the country of origin.

HEADLINE PUBLISHING GROUP LIMITED
An Hachette UK Company
Carmelite House
50 Victoria Embankment
London EC4Y 0DZ

The authorised representative in the EEA is Hachette Ireland, 8 Castlecourt Centre,
Dublin 15, D15 XTP3, Ireland (email: info@hbgi.ie)

www.headline.co.uk
www.hachette.co.uk